Alexander Hamilton's Economic Plan

Solving Problems in America's New Economy

Ryan P. Randolph

ROSEN CLASSROOM
PRIMARYSOURCE™

Rosen Classroom Books & Materials™
New York

Published in 2004 by The Rosen Publishing Group, Inc.
29 East 21st Street, New York, NY 10010

Copyright © 2004 by The Rosen Publishing Group, Inc.

First Edition

All rights reserved. No part of this book may be reproduced in any form without permission in writing from the publisher, except by a reviewer.

Library of Congress Cataloging-in-Publication Data

Randolph, Ryan P.
Alexander Hamilton's economic plan: solving problems in America's new economy / by Ryan Randolph.— 1st ed.
    p. cm. — (Life in the new American nation)
Includes bibliographical references and index.
ISBN 0-8239-4033-0 (library binding)
ISBN 0-8239-4251-1 (pbk. bdg.)
6-pack ISBN 0-8239-4264-3
1. United States—Economic policy. 2. Hamilton, Alexander, 1757–1804. 3. United States—History—1783-1815. I. Title. II. Series.
HC105 .R36 2004
330.973'04—dc21

2002152881

Manufactured in the United States of America

Cover (left): Alexander Hamilton
Cover (right): The Capitol in 1800

Photo credits: cover (left) © Bettmann/Corbis; cover (right), pp. 1, 5, 9, 13, 14, 17, 21 courtesy of the Library of Congress; p. 6 © AP/World Wide Photos; p. 19 © Hulton/Archive/Getty Images; pp. 25, 26 © Corbis.

Designer and Photo Researcher: Nelson Sá; Editor: Eliza Berkowitz

Contents

Introduction

Alexander Hamilton was an important founding father of the United States. If you have ever looked at a ten-dollar bill, you have seen a drawing of Alexander Hamilton. One reason he is important is that he explained to people in New York—and across America—that they should ratify, or approve, the U.S. Constitution. When he became the country's first secretary of the treasury, he set up an economic plan that fixed America's poor finances.

After America won its freedom from Great Britain in the Revolutionary War, it faced many problems. The United States had borrowed a lot of money from its citizens and foreign countries to fight the war. It now needed to pay back the money, but the young country did not have the funds to do so. Hamilton created a plan to pay what the United

States owed. His plans were very important in making the United States a strong nation.

There were three major parts of Hamilton's economic plan. First, the United States should pay foreign countries and U.S. citizens the money that the states owed. Second, a national bank should be established to control the making of paper money and to support the economy. Finally, the United States should focus on manufacturing, or making things such as ships, guns, and clothes. Hamilton did not want the United States to focus only on farming. If

Alexander Hamilton, pictured here, will forever be remembered as the first secretary of the treasury, an author of the Federalist Papers, and a delegate at the Constitutional Convention. His ideas helped the United States develop and maintain a financial plan. Hamilton helped the new country build a strong economy and start a national bank.

Americans did that, they would have to depend on other countries for manufactured goods.

When the Revolutionary War began in 1775, Hamilton left college to become the captain of an army

Alexander Hamilton worked as an aide to George Washington while Washington was the head of the Continental Army. Later, Washington was elected the first president of the United States. This print by James Merritt shows Hamilton (*left*) present at Washington's inauguration, which took place on April 30, 1789.

company in New York. He soon became an aide, or assistant, to George Washington. George Washington was the head of the Continental army. Hamilton was active in the army until October 1781, when the British surrendered at Yorktown. Many colonists viewed themselves as residents of a colony, not a union of states. Hamilton saw the United States as one country, not a loose group of colonies. After the war, Hamilton believed that the United States needed a strong national government. Other founding fathers, such as Thomas Jefferson, thought state governments should be stronger than the national government.

Chapter 1

The Constitution and Hamilton's Report on Public Credit

During the Revolutionary War, the Continental Congress, which represented all the colonies, passed the Articles of Confederation. The Articles of Confederation was a set of laws that created a national government. It did not give Congress much power. The new nation had a hard time raising money to pay back borrowed money.

In 1786, Hamilton was a member of the New York legislature. This legislature was a group of people who made laws. Hamilton proposed the Constitutional Convention for 1787 to help create a stronger national government. At the convention, Hamilton worked behind the scenes to make sure the new national government

The Articles of Confederation was the first Constitution of the United States. It was begun in 1776 and finished in 1777. The beginning of the document states: "To all to whom these Presents shall come, we the undersigned Delegates of the States affixed to our Names send greeting." The Articles of Confederation was replaced by the Consti-tution in 1789. The Constitution created a more powerful government for the new American nation.

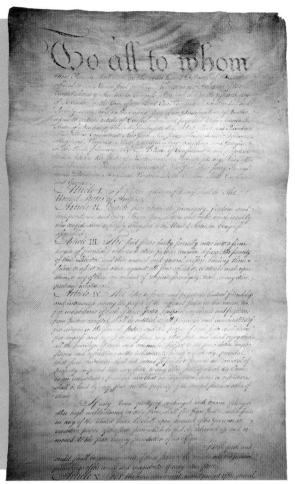

would be stronger. Some people did not agree with Hamilton. They thought a strong federal government would make the United States too much like Great Britain. Several compromises, or agreements between two opposite sides, were reached. Power was balanced between the states and the federal government. In 1788, voters approved the new Constitution of the United States.

Alexander Hamilton played an important role in convincing his home state, New York, to ratify the new Constitution. To help do this, Alexander Hamilton, John Jay, and James Madison wrote the Federalist Papers. These eighty-five essays provided short arguments on why the new Constitution would be good for the United States. Hamilton wrote most of these essays.

In 1789, George Washington was elected the first president of the United States. Alexander Hamilton was his secretary of the treasury. He knew that Hamilton could help the United States out of its financial problems.

The money that the United States had to pay back to the countries and people from which it borrowed is called debt. When the United States borrowed money, it issued a piece of paper known as a bond. The bonds said that the United States would pay the money back over a certain amount of time. If the United States did not pay back its debt, it would not have good credit. It would not be able to borrow money at a later time. Hamilton felt the United States would need to borrow money to help the country grow. He wanted to expand the small army and navy as well as industrial businesses.

Hamilton gave his plan to Congress in 1790. It was called the Report on Public Credit. Hamilton proposed that the United States first pay all debt owed to foreign countries. Second, Hamilton proposed the United States pay all of the debt to its citizens over time. Third, Hamilton wanted to take on the debts of the state governments. This meant the federal government would pay back the debts of the states.

The last part of Hamilton's report addressed how to fund the debt, or pay what the United States owed. He proposed that the government collect taxes to raise money. Items taxed should be luxury items such as wine, whiskey, coffee, tea, and many items coming from foreign countries.

Chapter 2

Opposition to Alexander Hamilton's Economic Plan

Not everybody agreed with Hamilton's plan to fix the economy. One founding father who disagreed with Hamilton was Thomas Jefferson. Jefferson was the main author of the Declaration of Independence. The Declaration of Independence said the United States was free from the British Empire. Jefferson went on to become the third president of the United States. James Madison was another opponent of Hamilton's plan. Madison wrote the Federalist Papers with Hamilton and later became the fourth president.

Hamilton wanted the federal government to take on all state debts. This way, the United States

This is a copy of the Declaration of Independence, written by Thomas Jefferson. The Declaration of Independence removed the United States from British control. It states that it had become "necessary for one people to dissolve the political bands which have connected them with another." This document was approved by Congress on July 4, 1776. The United States celebrates Independence Day on July 4 each year.

could make sure that states paid all the money they owed. Many states were against this plan, because some states, such as Virginia, had already paid all their debts. States that had already paid did not want to give money for states that had not paid their debts.

Hamilton proposed to pay U.S. citizens who held bonds, even if they did not originally buy them Many regular citizens, like farmers and veterans, originally

No. _____   Confederate States of America,

                                                    Office,

                                              _____186

THIS WILL CERTIFY That_____

has paid in at this Office_____

_____Dollars,

for which amount Registered Bonds of the Confederate States of America, bearing interest from this date, at the rate of four per cent. per annum, will be issued to him, under the "Act to reduce the currency, and to authorize a new issue of notes and bonds," approved February 17, 1864, upon the surrender of this Certificate at this office.

                              Depositary, C. S.

FOUR PER CENT. PER ANNUM

This is a treasury debt from 1864. It states that the bearer will gain 4 percent interest each year from the Confederate States of America. Bonds allowed people to essentially lend money to the U.S. government and be assured that they would get their money back, with an additional sum added.

lent money to the government. Some people could not wait for the government to pay back the debt. People who had enough money to take risks often bought the bonds from the original owners. These people were called speculators. They could take advantage of the fact that the government took its time to pay its debts. Speculators paid the farmers and veterans less money for their bonds, knowing that the government would pay the speculators back in full because they now owned that bond. Farmers and veterans that could not wait for the government took the money from the speculators in exchange for their bonds.

Madison and others thought it was unfair to the farmers who could not wait for the money. They also felt that more U.S. wealth, or money, was being put into the hands of a few rich people who could afford to buy bonds cheaply to make a profit. Madison proposed that original bondholders should be paid back in full, and speculators be paid less.

Hamilton realized that some people would lose money in his plan, and others would benefit. He knew

David Hume and other eighteenth-century economists from Scotland influenced Alexander Hamilton's economic plans. These economists studied the way the British and Dutch economies worked. Both governments had debts that were paid by gathering taxes. The debt supported economic growth and trade. National banks controlled the government's funds and made paper money so that people could trade, or buy and sell things easily.

that trying to track down original bondholders would be hard and take a long time. More important, he said that if current bondholders were not paid in full, they might not invest in the United States again. By paying the bondholders, even speculators, the United States would gain trust. This would help to create a strong economy for the future.

Hamilton wanted to make sure Congress adopted his proposals to pay back the United States's debt. He made a deal with his rival, Thomas Jefferson, and others who opposed him. Hamilton's friends in Congress voted with Jefferson's friends to move the U.S. capital from Philadelphia to Washington, D.C. In exchange, his opponents voted to assume the states' debt and pay all bondholders completely.

This is an image of the Capitol in Washington, D.C., from 1846. The Capitol has a rich history, including being the meeting place for the Supreme Court before the Supreme Court building was completed in 1935. The building itself has undergone many changes since it was originally built. Today, Congress meets in the Capitol .

At the time, Washington, D.C., was a swamp in part of Virginia near Maryland. Jefferson and others liked the idea of having the national government close to the southern states. This would put the government close to the farmers, whose interests might affect the laws that were made.

Chapter 3

The National Bank and Report on Manufactures

Hamilton also proposed creating a national bank to fund the finances of the country. The bank would serve a few purposes. It would hold the government's funds, make money for the whole country, make rules for other banks, and provide money to support businesses.

Jefferson, Madison, and many people in the southern United States opposed the national bank. They thought the national bank would not benefit farmers or the people who owned land—people like them. They thought only merchants and speculators would benefit from a national bank.

This 1799 engraving by William Russell Birch shows the first Bank of the United States. This building was located on Third Street in Philadelphia. Alexander Hamilton played a major role in urging those in power to open this bank. Once the Bank of the United States opened, it began issuing standard currency, or money, and dealing with the United States's debt from the Revolution.

Madison said that a national bank was not mentioned in the Constitution, so it was not legal to create it. President Washington considered rejecting the plan for the bank. He asked Hamilton for his view. Hamilton said the national bank was necessary to

The economic plan that Hamilton created alarmed Jefferson and Madison. It was not in the best interests of the landowners they represented, often in the southern states. They organized a political party against Hamilton and the merchants he represented, often in the North. Jefferson and Madison became leaders of the political party known as the Republicans (which was different from the Republican Party of today). Hamilton became a leader of the Federalist Party.

make the United States stronger. According to the Constitution, Congress could do what was "necessary and proper" to make sure the nation remained strong. Washington agreed with Hamilton, and the Bank of the United States was founded in 1791.

Hamilton finished his economic plan with the Report on Manufactures. It was a plan to help U.S. industry grow. The report proposed putting tariffs, or taxes, on foreign items that the United States wanted to make. The tariffs gave the government revenue, or money, to pay its debt. Tariffs would allow U.S. businesses to grow until they could compete with foreign businesses.

If there were no tariffs and people wanted fabrics, ships, or guns, they could be purchased

10. per cent on manuf. of flax, hemp, wool, cotton, silk, furs, or mixtures of

good, silver, copper, brass, iron, steel, tin, pewter

flour, salted beef, pork & fish, & oils

Except bar iron, bar lead, nails, spikes, steel unwrought

cables, cordage, yarn, twine, & pack thread.

15. do. on Porcelain, glass, stone, earthen wares.

50. do. on Spirits distilled from fruits

25. do. on Wines

free. in & out. grains, peas & other vegetables,

live cattle

pitch, tar, turpentine

unmanufactured wood

indigo, pot & pearl ash

flax, hemp, cotton, silk, wool

free out. & all raw materials

5. out. brown & clayed sugars.

~~————————~~ all non enumerated articles.

reciprocal. charges on vessels, cargoes, & merch. not within scope of above article

no bounties on goods to be exported to countries of other,

nor on ships it's own ships, or things imported in them.

no prohibns of any article of the other.

favors to others. to be common. on same condn.

no reduction of duty in favr of other nations but on consent of this.

The above contains Hamilton's tariff of the duties which cannot be received from on treaty with France, spoken of in my private note of Mar. 11. 92.

12597-

This is a photograph of a letter that Thomas Jefferson wrote to Alexander Hamilton on March 11, 1792. Jefferson did not like Hamilton's economic plan. At the time, both men were leaders of the two opposing political parties. Jefferson led the Anti-Federalists, whose main concern was states' rights. Hamilton led the Federalists, who favored a strong central government.

from other countries at a low price. In this case, the United States would rely on other countries for important items. For example, what if the United States bought ships from Britain instead of making them? If the United States were to go to war with Britain again, it could not defend itself against the British navy. The United States could not build its own ships and would not be able to get any from the British. Hamilton wanted to avoid this risk by building U.S. businesses. More businesses would also help the U.S. economy to grow.

The tariffs would make items made in the United States the same price or cheaper than foreign items. Hamilton proposed the tariffs so that the United States could build its own businesses and become more independent.

The Legacy of Alexander Hamilton and His Economic Plan

Chapter 4

Congress did not approve all of the Report on Manufactures, but it did set tariffs on certain foreign goods in 1792. This helped the new United States to build factories and businesses. Farming and raw materials also remained important parts of the U.S. economy.

Tariffs were the United States's largest source of revenue, or money, until the early 1900s. The United States and other countries still use tariffs, but less often. The United States now collects more money in income taxes from businesses and individuals than it does from tariffs.

The policy on tariffs and supporting new industries was only part of Hamilton's economic

Not even Alexander Hamilton was certain when he was born. It is believed that he was probably born in 1755 on the Caribbean island of Nevis. Nevis was a British colony as were the American colonies.

Hamilton had a tough childhood. His father, James Hamilton, left the family when Alexander was ten. Hamilton's mother, Rachel Faucett, died three years later. Soon after, Hamilton began working as a clerk for a local merchant, Nicholas Cruger. Hamilton impressed Cruger with his intelligence and hard work. Cruger and others raised money to send him to school in America. In 1774, Hamilton enrolled in King's College (known today as Columbia University) in New York.

Alexander Hamilton led an eventful life after serving as secretary of the treasury. He was active in national politics as part of the Federalist Party. He was also involved in several scandals.

On July 11, 1804, Alexander Hamilton was shot in a famous duel with Aaron Burr. Burr was the vice president of the United States. Hamilton died the day after the duel. Hamilton had played a role in making sure Thomas Jefferson became president over Aaron Burr in 1804. As a result, Burr challenged Hamilton to a duel, which Hamilton lost.

This portrait was created on July 11, 1804, the day of the famous duel between Aaron Burr and Alexander Hamilton. This duel took place in Weehawken, New Jersey, in the same place where Hamilton's son, Philip, was killed in a duel three years earlier. Burr and Hamilton had been enemies for a long time before Burr challenged Hamilton to this duel that ended Hamilton's life.

plan. It was combined with a plan to pay the national debt and to create a national bank. Today, the United States borrows billions of dollars from foreign countries and U.S. citizens. These investors (bondholders) buy and sell U.S. bonds and are confident that they will be paid back.

This photograph, taken by Irving Underhill in 1924, shows the New York branch of the Federal Reserve System. Since 1913, the Federal Reserve System has overseen banking in the United States. Without Alexander Hamilton's economic plan, the United States might have approached banking in a completely different way.

The national bank has a bumpy history in the United States. It was ended by President Andrew Jackson in the 1800s. The lack of a national bank to control the government's finances caused several financial panics. Today, the national bank is known as the Federal Reserve System. It was recreated in the 1920s. Like Hamilton's national bank, the Federal Reserve holds government funds, prints money, and makes rules for other banks.

At the beginning of the twenty-first century, the United States has the largest and strongest economy in the world. The United States was set on this path long ago by the financial plans created by Alexander Hamilton.

Glossary

Articles of Confederation (AR-tih-kuhls UV kuhn-feh-duh-RAY-shuhn) The first constitution of the United States, which lasted from March 1781 to June 1788.

bond (BAHND) An interest-bearing certificate issued by a government or company promising to pay the value of the certificate at a certain time.

credit (KREH-diht) Confidence in the ability of a person, company, or government to pay its debt.

debt (DET) Money owed to someone by a person, company, or government.

duel (DOO-el) Combat or fight between two people, ideas, or forces.

economy (ih-KAH-nuh-mee) The management of the finances and expenses of a government or household.

Federalist (FEH-duh-ruh-list) A member of a major political party in the early years of the

United States who favored a strong centralized national government.

finance (fi-NANTS) The system that includes granting credit, making investments, and circulating money.

industry (IN-duhs-tree) A group of productive or profit-making businesses.

legislature (LEH-jus-lay-cher) An organized group having the power to make laws.

manufacture (man-u-FAK-chur) To make a product by hand or machine from raw materials.

ratify (RAH-tih-fy) To approve or accept something.

Republican (ri-PUB-li-ken) A member of a political party in the early United States associated with farming and land interests who favored a restricted role for national government.

revenue (REH-vuh-noo) Money or income.

speculator (SPEK-yoo-lay-ter) Someone who makes a risky investment with hopes of a large gain.

tariff (TAR-if) A tax or duty imposed by a government on goods from another country.

Web Sites

Due to the changing nature of Internet links, the Rosen Publishing Group, Inc., has developed an online list of Web sites related to the subject of this book. This site is updated regularly. Please use this link to access the list:

http://www.rosenlinks.com/lnan/uscesc

Primary Source Image List

Page 1: Drawing by William Russell Birch. Created in 1827.
Page 5: Watercolor by D. W. C. Falls. Created in 1923. Housed in the National Archives and Records Administration.
Page 6: Print by James Merritt. Created in 1875. Housed in the collection of Currier & Ives Prints.
Page 9: The Articles of Confederation was adopted by the Continental Congress on November 15, 1777. Housed in the National Archives and Records Administration.
Page 13: The Declaration of Independence was adopted by Congress on July 4, 1776. Housed in the National Archives and Records Administration.
Page 14: Print created in 1864. Housed in the Ephemera Collection.
Page 17: Photograph by John Plumbe. Created in 1846. Housed in the Daguerreotype Collection.
Page 19: Engraving by William Russell Birch. Created in 1799.
Page 21: Papers written by Alexander Hamilton, dated March 11, 1792. Housed in the Thomas Jefferson Papers at the Library of Congress.
Page 26: Photograph by Irving Underhill. Created in 1924. Housed in the Museum of the City of New York.

Index

About the Author

Ryan P. Randoph is a freelance writer with an avid interest in history. Ryan has a bachelor of arts degree in both history and political science from Colgate University in Hamilton, New York. He has written several history books for children. He currently works for a consulting firm and lives with his wife in Mount Vernon, New York.